Read Me First: Password Protection and Identity Theft Prevention (2nd Edition)
ISBN 978-1490988870 (Print)
ISBN 978-0-9889810-3-4 (eBook)
Copyright © 2014 Institute for Education, Research, and Scholarships

All rights reserved. This work may not be translated or copied in whole or in part without the written permission of the publisher, except for brief excerpts in connection with reviews or scholarly analysis. Use in connection with any form of information storage and retrieval, electronic adaptation, computer software, or by similar or dissimilar methodology now known or hereafter developed is forbidden.

The use in this publication of trade names, trademarks, service marks, and similar terms, even if they are not identified as such, is not to be taken as an expression of opinion as to whether or not they are subject to proprietary rights. References to various copyrighted trademarks, characters, marks and registered marks may appear in this book. Rather than use a trademark symbol with every occurrence of a trademarked name, logo, or image we use the names, logos, and images only in an editorial fashion with no intention of infringement of the trademark.

This book is an independent publication by the Institute for Education, Research, and Scholarships.

Images used with permission and courtesy of Enrique Bosquet (p. 26), chanpipat (p. 6), ddpavumba (p. 16), emptyglass (p. 23), Victor Habbick (p. 20), Renjith Krishnan (p. 5), Stuart Miles (p. 18, 34, 36), Chris Sharp (p. 29), thanunkorn (p. 12), and Salvatore Vuono (cover, p. 9) from FreeDigitalPhotos.net.

# Contents

**CONTENTS** .................................................................................................. 2

**READ ME FIRST** ......................................................................................... 4

**CHAPTER 1: STOLEN PASSWORDS** ........................................................ 5

    1. More than a billion stolen usernames and passwords ........................... 5
    2. Two types of companies merging into one ............................................ 6

**CHAPTER 2: AVOIDING WEAK PASSWORDS** ......................................... 8
    1. Most passwords are weak ...................................................................... 8
    2. Most common passwords ...................................................................... 8

**CHAPTER 3: CREATING STRONG PASSWORDS** .................................. 10

    1. A strong password as a stem and a leaf .............................................. 10
    2. A strong password stem ...................................................................... 10
    3. A password leaf .................................................................................... 11
    4. Periodic password changes ................................................................. 11
    5. Safeguarding your strong passwords .................................................. 12

**CHAPTER 4: PASSWORD MANAGERS** .................................................. 13

    1. Password Managers ............................................................................. 13
    2. A Word of Caution ................................................................................ 13

**CHAPTER 5: ANSWERING PASSWORD SECURITY QUESTIONS** ....... 15

    1. The tinkerbell hack and Sarah Palin email hack ................................... 15
    2. How to answer password security questions ...................................... 15

**CHAPTER 6: DIVIDE AND CONQUER** ................................................... 17

    1. Handling a large number of passwords ............................................... 17
    2. Dividing online services into two security categories .......................... 17
    3. Strong passwords for secured websites .............................................. 18
    4. Two-factor authentication on secured websites .................................. 18
    5. Sharing a long password for unsecured websites ............................... 19

**CHAPTER 7: SMARTPHONE SECURITY** ............................................... 20

    1. Smartphones as part of the Internet ..................................................... 20
    2. Smartphone security checker ............................................................... 20

**CHAPTER 8: WIFI SECURITY** ..................................................................... 23
    *1. Google Street View* ............................................................................. 23
    *2. Public WiFi* ........................................................................................ 23
    *3. Home WiFi* ........................................................................................ 24

**CHAPTER 9: IDENTITY THEFT PREVENTION** ............................................... 25
    *1. Millions fall victim to identity theft* .................................................. 25
    *2. Identity theft awareness* ................................................................... 26
    *3. Fraud alert and credit freeze* ............................................................ 27
    *4. Social media* ..................................................................................... 28

**CHAPTER 10: EPILOGUE** ........................................................................... 29
**BIBLIOGRAPHY** ........................................................................................ 31
**INDEX** ..................................................................................................... 36
**ABOUT THE AUTHOR** .............................................................................. 39

# Read Me First

More than a billion online usernames and passwords have been stolen by cybercriminals. Chances are that some of your passwords are already in the wrong hands.

Password protection is more than meets the eye. This booklet offers you step-by-step instructions in creating strong passwords that are easy for you to remember but difficult for hackers to crack. It also tells you how to properly handle password security questions as well as smartphone and WiFi security.

In 2012, the Verizon RISK (Response, Intelligence, Solutions, Knowledge) Team released a Data Breach Investigations Report in cooperation with the Australian Federal Police (AFP), Dutch National High Tech Crime Unit (NHTCU), Irish Reporting and Information Security Service (IRISS), U.K. Police Central e-Crime Unit (PCeU), and U.S. Secret Service (USSS). Two of the most significant findings are [1]:

1. 96 % of cyber attacks were unsophisticated.
2. 97 % of breaches were avoidable through simple security measures such as firewalls and strong password protection.

Most firewalls are free and no-brainer to install. Strong password protection, however, requires some thinking and planning. This booklet will assist you in creating strong passwords.

The booklet also reveals the most effective method for identity theft prevention. Every year, more than 12 million Americans have fallen victim to identity fraud [2]. I was one of them many years ago. You do not want to take the chance of becoming a victim. This booklet shows you a simple preemptive measure to protect yourself and your family.

If you have any questions after reading this booklet, please send an email to books@ifers.org

# Chapter 1: Stolen Passwords

## 1. More than a billion stolen usernames and passwords

More than a billion online usernames and passwords have been stolen by cybercriminals. Chances are that some of your passwords are already in the wrong hands. Here are some of the recent high-profile password breaches:

1. In 2009, online games service company RockYou suffered a data breach that resulted in the exposure of over 32 million usernames and passwords [3]. RockYou stored passwords in plain text format without any encryption.
2. In 2011, cybercriminals breached the database of online dating site PlentyofFish.com, exposing the personal and password information on nearly 30 million users [4].
3. In 2012, cybercriminals stole 6.5 million LinkedIn passwords and posted them on an online forum [5]. LinkedIn passwords were encoded using SHA-1 — a cryptographic hash function with weak collision resistance.
4. In 2012, Yahoo! Voices was hacked, resulting in the theft of 450,000 customer usernames and passwords [6].
5. In 2013, cybercriminals accessed Twitter user data and stole the usernames, email addresses, session tokens, and encrypted/salted versions of passwords for approximately 250,000 users [7].
6. In 2013, cybercriminals gained access to cloud-storage service provider Evernote's user information, including usernames, email addresses, and encrypted passwords of its 50 million users [8].
7. In 2014, Hold Security revealed that a Russian crime ring has stolen a massive 1.2 billion username/password combinations and more than 500 million email addresses from 420,000 websites.

"Hackers did not just target U.S. companies, they targeted any website they could get, ranging from Fortune 500 companies to very small websites," said Alex Holden, founder and chief information security officer of Hold Security. "And most of these sites are still vulnerable" [9].

8. In 2014, Apple's iCloud online data backup service might have been compromised by cybercriminals who stole and shared publicly nude selfies of Jennifer Lawrence, Kirsten Dunst, Kate Upton, Mary Elizabeth Winstead, and other celebrities. Apple claimed that the celebrity accounts "were compromised by a very targeted attack on usernames, passwords and security questions" [10].

9. In 2014, cybercriminals who called themselves the Guardians of Peace (GOP) stole 100 terabytes of data [11], destroyed 75% of corporate computer servers, and crippled the company's data centers [12] at Sony Pictures. Among the stolen data were five feature films, executive emails, business contracts, company budgets, employee personal data, salary information, medical records, and celebrity secrets [13].

## 2. Two types of companies merging into one

For every publicized data breach incident, there are hundreds of undisclosed security breaches. Although Apple, Facebook, Twitter, and some other organizations have come forward in reporting cyber attacks [14], the vast majority of companies refuse to confirm news reports of online attacks due to their fear of the stock market volatility and the loss of consumer confidence. The list of companies includes the International Olympic Committee, Exxon Mobil, Baker Hughes, Royal Dutch Shell, BP, ConocoPhillips, Chesapeake Energy, the British energy giant BG Group, the steel maker ArcelorMittal, and Coca-Cola [15].

Federal Bureau of Investigation (FBI) director Robert Mueller said in 2012, "There are only two types of companies: those that have been hacked, and those that will be. Even that is merging into one category: those that have been hacked and will be again" [16].

Computer security executive Dmitri Alperovitch added, "I divide the entire set of Fortune Global 2000 firms into two categories: those that know they've been compromised and those that don't yet know" [15].

Fortunately, most companies nowadays encrypt their customer's passwords with strong cryptography. If you employ strong passwords, you have less to worry about cybercriminals cracking the stolen password lists from those companies. For other online companies that do not properly safeguard their customer databases, we are at the mercy of the unscrupulous hackers. This booklet presents the practical preemptive measures that you can implement today to protect yourself and your family.

# Chapter 2: Avoiding Weak Passwords

## 1. Most passwords are weak

A 2009 article in the *Proceedings of the Human Factors and Ergonomics Society* cited a survey of 836 people about their password usage and behavior. The survey showed that [17]:
1. 18 % of respondents always use the same password to access multiple computers and websites.
2. 44 % of respondents use a short password (less than 8 characters).
3. 44 % of respondents write their passwords down on a piece of paper or a document file.

Microsoft's security guru Jesper Johansson explained the prevalence of weak passwords: "How many have [a] password policy that says under penalty of death you shall not write down your password? I claim that is absolutely wrong. I claim that password policy should say you should write down your password. I have 68 different passwords. If I am not allowed to write any of them down, guess what I am going to do? I am going to use the same password on every one of them. Since not all systems allow good passwords, I am going to pick a really crappy one, use it everywhere and never change it" [18].

## 2. Most common passwords

In 2012, CNet analyzed the most frequently used passwords that were cracked by cybercriminals in the Yahoo! Voices data breach. Among more than 450,000 stolen login credentials, the most common passwords in descending order of popularity were [19]:
1. 123456

2. password
3. 111111
4. welcome
5. ninja
6. freedom
7. f*ck
8. baseball
9. superman
10. 000000
11. America
12. winner
13. starwars
14. batman
15. spiderman
16. lakers
17. maverick
18. ncc1701
19. startrek,
20. ncc1701a

One may expect that advanced computer users are better with password protection. However, *Ars Technica* revealed a disturbing observation: "Experience made a difference, as expert and advanced computer users tended to outperform the novices. But there were limits; actual network administrators, for example, didn't behave in a manner that was significantly different from an average user" [20].

Indeed, the 2012 Data Breach Investigations Report by the Verizon RISK (Response, Intelligence, Solutions, Knowledge) Team indicated that 94 % of all data compromised involved servers [1]. Many network administrators are not doing enough to prevent computer server intrusions.

A 2013 article in *Ars Technica* describes in detail how easy it is for hackers to crack weak passwords using only free tools and resources on the Internet [21]. Weak passwords include dictionary words, popular phrases, celebrity names, and strings of numbers or characters that are easy to guess.

# Chapter 3: Creating Strong Passwords

## 1. A strong password as a stem and a leaf

A strong password is consisted of a strong stem and a comparatively weaker leaf as though it were a biological plant. The same stem with different leaves creates similar but unique strong passwords. You can then use a different strong password for each and every secured website.

The stem-leaf password system is based on a commercial implementation of RSA SecurID system in which a password/RSA SecurID code combination is used to log on to a server. The RSA SecurID code changes at fixed intervals (e.g. 30 seconds) using a built-in clock and a random number generator specific to a device (aka token) that the user carries in person.

Since everyday users do not have access to RSA SeucrID, a stem-leaf password approach is more appropriate.

## 2. A strong password stem

To come up with a strong password stem, avoid dictionary words, acronyms, abbreviations, popular phrases, celebrity names, and strings of numbers or characters that are easy to guess. A strong password stem should be at least 8 characters long with a combination of alphabets (upper and lowercase), numbers (0-9), and special characters (e.g. !, @, #, $, %, ^, &, *). Nevertheless, the password stem should easy for you to remember so that it does not need to be written down anywhere.

For a married couple, a strong password stem can be constructed from the couple's real names, nicknames, hobbies, interests, and special events. For instance, if Jack calls his wife Jill by her nickname "Betty Boop" and they had a Disneyland wedding in the summer of 2008, a strong password stem can be "J&B@di08."

Take another example, a student whose ambition is to become the president of the United States (POTUS) by age 30 can create a strong password stem as "pot$US30."

Use the password stem and combine it with a password leaf (see the section below) to create a unique strong password that is at least 12 characters long.

## 3. A password leaf

A password leaf is appended to a strong password stem in order to create a unique strong password for each secured website. Do *not* use the same password leaf across multiple sites.

To come up with a password leaf, tap into your associative memory. Take the example of the married couple Jack and Jill: Suppose they opened a joint bank account on the same week when they adopted a puppy from an animal shelter. A password leaf can be based on the name of their puppy, say, "Cookie." Therefore, a strong password for Jack and Jill's joint bank account is "J&B@di08Coo#kie."

Take another example of the student whose ambition is to become the president of the United States: She checks the daily horoscope delivered to her email box every day. A password leaf can be based on her astrological sign, say, "Pisces." Therefore, a strong password for her email account is "pot$US30Pis&ces."

## 4. Periodic password changes

Some secured websites require users to change their passwords periodically, such as once every 60 days. You can easily change a strong password by either replacing the password leaf or adjusting the password stem.

If you adjust the password stem, you may want to change your passwords on all the secured websites in order to avoid the confusion of having multiple password stems.

For instance, "J&B@di08Coo#kie" can be changed to: "J&B@di08C+ookie" (leaf replacement) or "J&Bdi08%Coo#kie" (stem adjustment).
Likewise, "pot$US30Pis&ces" can be changed to: "pot$US30Fi+shes" (leaf replacement) or "3$0potus$Pis&ces" (stem adjustment).

## 5. Safeguarding your strong passwords

Microsoft's security guru Jesper Johansson recommended people to jot down their passwords [18]. However, strong passwords become useless if someone else gets hold of that piece of paper or electronic document that stores your passwords.

If you follow the step-by-step instructions in this chapter, you will probably remember many if not all your strong passwords, one for each secured website. Nonetheless, if you must write down your passwords, you can safeguard your password list by:

1. Using shorthand to abbreviate the strong passwords. For example, "J&B@di08Coo#kie" can be jotted down as "J..@..C" whereas "pot$US30Pis&ces" can be written as "p..$..Pi."
2. Encrypting the electronic document that contains the abbreviated passwords. Create one strong password that you will never forget and use that to encrypt the document.

# Chapter 4: Password Managers

## 1. Password Managers

Some security experts suggest using a secure password manager such as LastPass, 1Password, and KeePass to create a long, strong, and different password for each and every website that requires a login password.

The main advantage of using a password manager is that you only need to create one strong "master" password that you can remember. The password manager would automate password generation and form filling for you.

LastPass, for instance, is available as a free plugin for many popular web browsers including Internet Explorer, Firefox, Chrome, and Safari. For paid subscribers, LastPass offers additional protection such as entering your password using your mouse on a virtual screen keyboard to protect yourself from keyloggers and keysniffers.

To come up with a strong "master" password, you can follow the stem-leaf approach described in Chapter 3.

## 2. A Word of Caution

If that one single "master" password is ever compromised, all your passwords are no longer secure. Therefore, it is utmost important to create a strong password for use as the master password in the password manager such as LastPass.

In May 2011, cybercriminals breached the LastPass servers and possibly stole email addresses of users, the server salt, and the salted password hashes from the LastPass database [22]. LastPass responded quickly and notified their users to change their master passwords as a precaution. The company subsequently improved their server security and rolled out PBKDF2 (Password-Based Key Derivation Function 2) using

SHA-256 (a SHA-2 Secure Hash Algorithm) on their servers with a 256-bit salt utilizing 100,000 rounds.

Designed by the National Security Agency (NSA), SHA-2 is significantly better than its predecessor SHA-1 — a cryptographic hash function with weak collision resistance. In June 2012, cybercriminals stole 6.5 million LinkedIn passwords and posted them on an online forum [5]. Since the LinkedIn passwords were encoded using SHA-1, about half of the encrypted passwords have been decrypted and posted online.

In spite of tightened security measures, cyber attackers compromised LastPass servers again in June 2015, stealing hashed user passwords, cryptographic salts, password reminders, and email addresses [23].

# Chapter 5: Answering Password Security Questions

## 1. The tinkerbell hack and Sarah Palin email hack

In September 2008, 20-year-old college student David Kernell hacked into Republican vice presidential candidate Sarah Palin's Yahoo! email account to look for information that would derail her campaign [24]. Kernell managed to reset Palin's account password by entering her birth date and correctly answering the security question "Where did you meet your spouse?" It only took Kernell 45 minutes on Wikipedia and Google search to find the correct answer.

There is also the infamous "tinkerbell hack" that refers to Paris Hilton's T-mobile account hack [25]. The attacker was able to answer Hilton's password reset security question, "What is the name of your pet?" The answer was simple: "Tinkerbell."

## 2. How to answer password security questions

To prevent someone from hacking into your online account through password security questions, do *not* ever answer the online security questions straightforwardly. Instead, treat each security answer as a long password or simply be creative. Here are some good examples:

1. Question: Where did you meet your spouse?
   Answer: lunchvtmay1980 (Meaning: During lunch at Virginia Tech in May 1980)
2. Question: What was the name of your first school?
   Answer: vanillaicecreamsmell (Meaning: Your first school reminds you of the smell of Vanilla ice cream.)

3. Question: What is your pet's name?
   Answer: squarerootofminus1 (Meaning: Since the square root of minus 1 is an imaginary number, you don't have a pet or perhaps you have an imaginary pet.)
4. Question: What is your pet's name?
   Answer: saturdaynightlive1979skit (Meaning: You do have a pet who reminds you of a skit in a 1979 TV show "Saturday Night Live.")

# Chapter 6: Divide and Conquer

## 1. Handling a large number of passwords

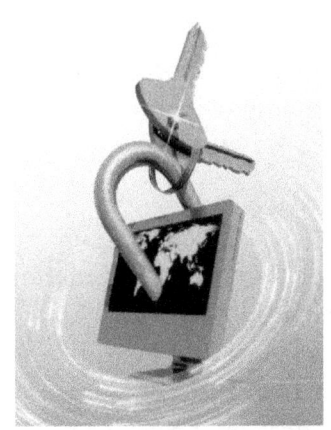

Amazon Top 500 reviewer and business consultant Ethan A. Winning argues that the stem-leaf password system (Chapter 3) cannot help us remember the tens if not hundreds of passwords that we ultimately have to come up with in our daily lives. Using a password manager (Chapter 4) is one possible solution. However, if we do not want to use a password manager to handle a large number of passwords, the answer is to divide and conquer.

## 2. Dividing online services into two security categories

You can rest assured that your banks and credit card companies employ strong encryption on all their customers' usernames and passwords. Therefore, strong passwords will keep you safe even if cybercriminals are able to steal the databases from those companies.

However, the same cannot be said for many other online websites. In 2009, online games service company RockYou suffered a data breach that resulted in the exposure of over 32 million usernames and passwords [3]. RockYou stored passwords in plain text format without any encryption.

*Beware of unsecured websites!* A website is unsecure if:

(a) The website ever emails you your login name and password in plain text, OR

(b) The website uses **http:** instead of **https:** (Hypertext Transfer Protocol Secure) during your sign-up or login process.

After you have divided the online services into two security categories (secured and unsecured), use a unique strong password for each of the secured sites, and use a shared long password for all the unsecured sites.

If you still have too many websites in the secured category, you may consider moving the unimportant sites to the unsecured category. An unimportant website is one that contains no personal information and that you do not mind reregistering for a new username when necessary.

## 3. Strong passwords for secured websites

Use a strong password for every secured website. Chapter 3 (Creating Strong Passwords) shows you how to create strong passwords that are easy for you to remember but difficult for hackers to crack.

Do *not* use the same strong password across different secured websites unless you turn on two-factor authentication on all of those sites (see the following section).

## 4. Two-factor authentication on secured websites

Turn on two-factor authentication on Google, Facebook, Dropbox, Apple iCloud, Twitter, Microsoft, and other websites that offer such security functionality [26]. You will need your username, password, and a code that a website sends to your cell phone in order for you to access the website.

As Google explains, "2-step verification drastically reduces the chances of having the personal information in your Google Account stolen by someone else. Why? Because bad guys would have to not only get your password and your username, they'd have to get a hold of your phone" [27].

To set up 2-step verification on Google, log into Google+, then go to https://www.google.com/settings/security. For Facebook, first log in, then go to https://www.facebook.com/settings?tab=security and select the "Login Approvals" security setting.

## 5. Sharing a long password for unsecured websites

*Avoid creating passwords on unsecured websites if possible.* If you have no choice but to create a password on an unsecured website, do *not* reuse the same or similar strong password that you use on the secured websites. Otherwise, you risk exposing your strong passwords to cybercriminals.

Instead, use a long password: at least 12 characters with a combination of alphabets, numbers, and special characters. Avoid dictionary words, acronyms, abbreviations, popular phrases, celebrity names, and strings of numbers or characters that are easy to guess. Nevertheless, the password should be easy for you to remember so that it does not need to be written down anywhere. An example of a long password is iwant2b#actor18! ("i want to be an actor when I turn 18").

# Chapter 7: Smartphone Security

## 1. Smartphones as part of the Internet

"Your cell phone is communicating completely digital; it's part of the Internet," said Army Gen. Keith Alexander, director of the National Security Agency (NSA) and commander of the U.S. Cyber Command. "The attack surfaces for adversaries to get on the Internet now include all those mobile devices. ... The mobile security situation lags. It's far behind" [28].

The current design of mobile devices makes differentiating legitimate sites from malicious ones a tricky task. "No matter how tantalizing a link might look on a desktop, there are cues that you shouldn't go there, such as an address that just doesn't look safe," said Hugh Thompson, Blue Coat's senior vice president and chief security strategist. "When you click a link on a mobile phone, it's harder to know what form of Russian roulette they're playing" [29].

In February 2012, technology and market research company Forrester Research estimated that one billion people will own smartphones by 2016 [30]. These mobile phones are powerful little computers that are always on, 24/7. Consequently, they are the perfect targets for cybercriminals. Indeed, cyber attacks on mobile phones rose by a whopping 500 % in 2012, according to McAfee [31].

## 2. Smartphone security checker

The Federal Communications Commission (FCC) has released a "Smartphone Security Checker" to help consumers secure their mobile devices [32]. The FCC website is http://www.fcc.gov/smartphone-security

The FCC website provides specific security checkers for Android, Apple iOS, BlackBerry, and Windows Phone. The general security checklist is as follows:

1. Set PINs and passwords to prevent unauthorized access to your phone. Configure your phone to automatically lock after five minutes or less when your phone is idle, as well as use the SIM password capability available on most smartphones.
2. Do not modify your smartphone's security settings. Tampering with your phone's factory settings, jailbreaking, or rooting your phone undermines the built-in security features offered by your wireless service and smartphone, while making it more susceptible to an attack.
3. Backup and secure all of the data stored on your phone.
4. Only install mobile apps from trusted sources.
5. Understand app permissions before accepting them. Be cautious about granting applications access to personal information on your phone or otherwise letting the application have access to perform functions on your phone.
6. Install anti-theft security protection apps that enable remote location and wiping. Some carriers offer a free "remote wipe" service that allows users to delete all of the data from a lost or stolen device to prevent data or identity theft. You cannot rely solely on passcode to protect your smartphone's content. It was discovered in January 2013 that a security flaw in Apple's iOS 6.1 allows anyone to bypass your iPhone password lock [33].
7. Keep your phone's software up-to-date by enabling automatic updates or accepting updates when prompted from your service provider, operating system provider, device manufacturer, or application provider.
8. Be smart on open Wi-Fi networks. When you access a public Wi-Fi network, your phone can be an easy target of cybercriminals. Always be aware when clicking on web links and be particularly cautious if you are asked to enter account or login information.
9. Wipe data on your old phone before you donate, resell, or recycle it. To protect your privacy, completely erase data off of your phone and reset the phone to its initial factory settings.

10. Report a stolen smartphone. The major wireless service providers, in coordination with the FCC, have established a stolen phone database. This will provide notice to all the major wireless service providers that the phone has been stolen and will allow for remote "bricking" of the phone so that it cannot be activated on any wireless network without your permission.

# Chapter 8: WiFi Security

## 1. Google Street View

Google Street View is amazingly useful for everyone who uses Google Maps. However, Google disclosed in May 2010 that for over three years, its camera-toting Street View cars have inadvertently collected snippets of private information that people send over unencrypted WiFi networks [34].

In October 2010, Google admitted to accidentally collecting and storing entire e-mails, URLs, and passwords from unsecured WiFi networks with its Street View cars in more than 30 countries, including the United States, Canada, Mexico, some of Europe, and parts of Asia [35].

Alan Eustace, Google's senior vice president of engineering and research, wrote in the Google Public Policy Blog, "It's clear from those inspections that while most of the data is fragmentary, in some instances entire emails and URLs were captured, as well as passwords. We want to delete this data as soon as possible, and I would like to apologize again for the fact that we collected it in the first place" [36].

It was an honest mistake by Google. The same cannot be said for cybercriminals who troll the neighborhoods for WiFi signals.

## 2. Public WiFi

Public WiFi at coffee shops and department stores are inherently unsecure even if they require a password to connect. Do *not* send any unencrypted sensitive data using public WiFi because the transmission can be easily intercepted by a third party including cybercriminals. Surfing the web on public WiFi is okay, but avoid doing online banking or emailing personal information over public WiFi.

In 2007, cybercriminals intercepted wireless transfers of customer information at two Miami-area Marshalls stores; and 10 people were convicted in Florida for their roles in a ring using stolen TJX customer data to buy gift cards and merchandise [37].

## 3. Home WiFi

When you install a private WiFi network router at home, be certain to:
1. Change the router's administrative password from the factory default to a strong password.
2. Enable wireless authentication and encryption WPA/WPA2 AES.
3. Assign a strong password to the WPA Pre-Shared Key (WPA-PSK) or WPA2 Pre-Shared Key (WPA2-PSK).

To change the administrative password on a network router, type in the web address http://192.168.0.1/ or http://192.168.1.1/ depending on the manufacturer's specifications. Typically, the router's default username is "admin" and the default password is "password." Once you have logged in, you should change the default password to a strong password. Some routers also allow you to change the administrative username in addition to the password.

In configuring the home wireless network, enable WPA2-PSK if available or enable WPA-PSK only if WPA2-PSK is unavailable. WPA2 (Wireless Protected Access 2) improves the security of WiFi connections using stronger wireless encryption than WPA (Wireless Protected Access).

The WPA/WPA2 encryption mode should be set to AES instead of TKIP if possible. Compared to TKIP (Temporal Key Integrity Protocol), AES (Advanced Encryption Standard) is a better encryption technology.

Finally, assign a strong password to the WPA Pre-Shared Key (WPA-PSK) or WPA2 Pre-Shared Key (WPA2-PSK).

# Chapter 9: Identity Theft Prevention

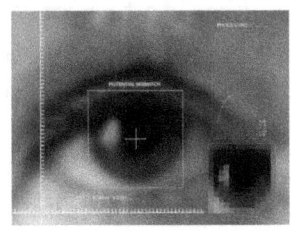

## 1. Millions fall victim to identity theft

In 2012, more than 12.6 million Americans were victims of identity fraud [38]. NBC News reported in February 2013 that "a large portion of the increase was driven by 'dramatic jumps' in more-serious forms of ID theft, such as new account fraud, where a criminal uses a victim's personal information to open new credit cards or other kinds of loans. New account fraud jumped 50 % last year, with the total fraud loss doubling year over year to just under $10 billion" [38].

I was one of the victims years ago. In attempt to find the best mortgage deal, I disclosed to several brokers my personal information including social security number, copy of my driver license, and bank statements. A few months later, an identity thief opened a new online bank account in my name, and transferred money from my bank to his own account. Over the years, several of my coworkers have also fallen victim to identity theft.

In 2014, cybercriminals sole 4.5 million names, social security numbers, physical addresses, birthdays, and telephone numbers from Community Health Systems that operates 206 hospitals across the United States. *CNN* reported, "Anyone who received treatment from a physician's office tied to a network-owned hospital in the last five years -- or was merely referred there by an outside doctor -- is affected. The large data breach puts these people at heightened risk of identity fraud. That allows criminals open bank accounts and credit cards on their behalf, take out loans and ruin personal credit history" [39].

Despite the massive data breaches and surge in identity theft, we can protect ourselves better than before.

## 2. Identity theft awareness

The Federal Trade Commission (FTC) has issued this important advice: "Awareness is an effective weapon against many forms of identity theft. Be aware of how information is stolen and what you can do to protect yours, monitor your personal information to uncover any problems quickly, and know what to do when you suspect your identity has been stolen" [40].

In specific, we must all take the following steps to deter identity thieves, detect suspicious activity, and defend against identity theft. Based on the FTC recommendations, you can:

1. Deter identity thieves by safeguarding your information:

(a) Shred financial documents and paperwork with personal information before you discard them.

(b) Sign up for paperless statements from your banks and utility companies.

(c) Do not carry your Social Security card or write your Social Security number on a check.

(d) Use strong passwords on secured websites and long passwords on unsecured websites.

(e) Set a passcode or password on your smartphone for protection.

(f) Keep the anti-virus software up-to-date on your computers.

(g) Do not access sensitive information or install any software through public WiFi or Internet connections in hotels, restaurants, and other public venues. (The FBI issued a warning on May 8, 2012 about travelers' laptops being infected with malicious software while using hotel Internet connections [41].)

(h) Opt out pre-screened credit and insurance offers to prevent potential thieves from intercepting and accepting the offers in your name. Opting out can be done online at https://www.optoutprescreen.com/

2. Detect suspicious activity by monitoring your information:
>(a) Review financial accounts and billing statements regularly.
>(b) Examine your Google Account Activity for any suspicious activities with your account sign-ins, visited places, emails, web history, etc [42].
>(c) Set up Google Alerts at http://www.google.com/alerts to monitor the web 24/7 for any news and videos about you or someone with the same name as you [43]. You can receive an alert once a week, once a day, or as-it-happens.
>(d) Obtain your free annual credit reports from TransUnion, Equifax, and Experian; and look for abnormalities or inaccuracies.

3. Defend against identity theft by proactive measures:
>(a) Place a fraud alert and a credit freeze on your credit reports at TransUnion, Equifax, and Experian. Fraud alerts and credit freeze help prevent an identity thief from opening new financial accounts, applying for loans, and seeking employment in your name.
>(d) Report all identity theft incidences to the police and the FTC at 1-877-ID-THEFT.

## 3. Fraud alert and credit freeze

The most effective method to protect yourself from identity theft is to place a fraud alert *and* a credit freeze on your credit reports at TransUnion, Equifax, and Experian.

Fraud alerts and credit freezes together prevent identity thieves from opening new financial accounts, applying for loans, and seeking employment in your name.

When you need to conduct business that requires a credit check, you will simply contact TransUnion, Equifax, and Experian to temporarily lift the credit freezes for a short period of time or to make the information available only to a specific requester.

**To add a fraud alert on your credit reports, contact:**
1. TransUnion:

http://www.transunion.com/personal-credit/credit-disputes/fraud-alerts.page

2. Equifax:
https://www.alerts.equifax.com/AutoFraud_Online/jsp/fraudAlert.jsp

3. Experian:
https://www.experian.com/fraud/center.html

**To place a credit freeze on your credit reports, contact:**

1. TransUnion:
http://www.transunion.com/personal-credit/credit-disputes/credit-freezes.page

2. Equifax:
https://www.freeze.equifax.com/Freeze/jsp/SFF_PersonalIDInfo.jsp

3. Experian:
http://www.experian.com/consumer/security_freeze.html

Credit freezes work really well. A few years ago, I went to an upscale auto dealership to test drive a car. I told the salesman that I needed to give it some thoughts but he was persistent in selling me the car and checking my credit scores right away. I informed him that I had credit freezes and I was not ready to make a purchase decision on the spot. He said, "No problem, just fill in the application form, my manager has a way to check your credit scores." To be polite, I obliged. Then he took the completed application to his manager's office. After a few minutes, he returned with an agitated expression on his face and uttered in disbelief, "You don't exist!"

Your nonexistence in the eye of criminals eliminates you as a potential target of fraud and financial crimes.

## 4. Social media

Beware of how much personal information you divulge in social media such as Facebook, LinkedIn, Twitter, and other websites. You should use their privacy settings to restrict public access to your personal information and pictures that are meant for only friends and families.

For more information about social media and privacy, check out my 2014 book *Facebook Nation: Total Information Awareness* (2nd Edition, ISBN 978-1-4939-1739-6) published by Springer Science+Business Media [44].

# Chapter 10: Epilogue

This booklet has dived into some details of password protection, smartphone security, WiFi security, and identity theft prevention. Akin to a horror movie that leaves a glimpse of an unknown future at the end of a seemingly happy ending, I end the booklet with a heart-wrenching story about the security flaws in customer services that led to a devastating hack into *Wired* technology journalist Mat Honan in August 2012:

"In the space of one hour, my entire digital life was destroyed. First my Google account was taken over, then deleted. Next my Twitter account was compromised, and used as a platform to broadcast racist and homophobic messages. And worst of all, my AppleID account was broken into, and my hackers used it to remotely erase all of the data on my iPhone, iPad, and MacBook.

"Getting into Amazon let my hackers get into my Apple ID account, which helped them get into Gmail, which gave them access to Twitter. ... But what happened to me exposes vital security flaws in several customer service systems, most notably Apple's and Amazon's. Apple tech support gave the hackers access to my iCloud account. Amazon tech support gave them the ability to see a piece of information — a partial credit card number — that Apple used to release information. In short, the very four digits that Amazon considers unimportant enough to display in the clear on the web are precisely the same ones that Apple considers secure enough to perform identity verification. The disconnect exposes flaws in data management policies endemic to the entire technology industry, and points to a looming nightmare as we enter the era of cloud computing and connected devices" [45].

Mat Honan's story reminds all of us that cybersecurity is everyone's responsibility – individuals, companies, and governments.

For more information about protecting yourself from phishing, spoofing, and other cyber attacks, please check out my book *Counterterrorism and Cybersecurity: Total Information Awareness* (ISBN 978-3-319-17243-9) published by Springer Science+Business Media in April 2015 [46].

# Bibliography

[1] Verizon RISK Team, "2012 Data Breach Investigations Report," Verizon, 2012. [Online]. Available: http://www.verizonbusiness.com/resources/reports/rp_data-breach-investigations-report-2012_en_xg.pdf.

[2] Javelin Strategy & Research, "More Than 12 Million Identity Fraud Victims in 2012 According to Latest Javelin Strategy & Research Report," Javelin Strategy & Research, 20 February 2013. [Online]. Available: https://www.javelinstrategy.com/news/1387/92/1.

[3] N. Cubrilovic, "RockYou Hack: From Bad To Worse," TechCrunch, 14 December 2009. [Online]. Available: http://techcrunch.com/2009/12/14/rockyou-hack-security-myspace-facebook-passwords/.

[4] B. Krebs, "PlentyofFish.com Hacked, Blames Messenger," KrebsOnSecurity.com, 31 January 2011. [Online]. Available: http://krebsonsecurity.com/2011/01/plentyoffish-com-hacked-blames-messenger/.

[5] D. Goldman, "More than 6 million LinkedIn passwords stolen," CNNMoney, 7 June 2012. [Online]. Available: http://money.cnn.com/2012/06/06/technology/linkedin-password-hack/index.htm.

[6] D. Gross, "Yahoo hacked, 450,000 passwords posted online," CNN, 13 July 2012. [Online]. Available: http://www.cnn.com/2012/07/12/tech/web/yahoo-users-hacked/index.html?hpt=hp_t1.

[7] B. Lord, "Keeping our users secure," Twitter Blog, 1 February 2013. [Online]. Available: http://blog.twitter.com/2013/02/keeping-our-users-secure.html.

[8] D. Engberg, "Security Notice: Service-wide Password Reset," The Evernote Blog, 2 March 2013. [Online]. Available: http://blog.evernote.com/blog/2013/03/02/security-notice-service-wide-password-reset/.

[9] N. Perlroth and D. Gelles, "Russian Hackers Amass Over a Billion Internet Passwords," The New York Times, 5 August 2014. [Online]. Available: http://www.nytimes.com/2014/08/06/technology/russian-gang-said-to-

amass-more-than-a-billion-stolen-internet-credentials.html.

[10] C. Cooper, "Celebs, beware: Those nude selfies will be hacked and shared," CNet, 2 September 2014. [Online]. Available: http://www.cnet.com/news/the-new-price-of-celebrity-careful-before-taking-that-nudie-selfie/.

[11] A. C. Estes, "The Sony Pictures Hack Was Even Worse Than Everyone Thought," GIZMODO, 3 December 2014. [Online]. Available: http://gizmodo.com/the-sony-pictures-hack-exposed-budgets-layoffs-and-3-1665739357/1666122168/+ace.

[12] M. Cieply and B. Barnes, "Sony Cyberattack, First a Nuisance, Swiftly Grew Into a Firestorm," The New York Times, 30 December 2014. [Online]. Available: http://www.nytimes.com/2014/12/31/business/media/sony-attack-first-a-nuisance-swiftly-grew-into-a-firestorm-.html.

[13] K. Zetter, "Sony Hackers Threaten to Release a Huge 'Christmas Gift' of Secrets," Wired, 15 December 2014. [Online]. Available: http://www.wired.com/2014/12/sony-hack-part-deux/.

[14] D. Gross, "Report: Eastern European gang hacked Apple, Facebook, Twitter," CNN, 20 February 2013. [Online]. Available: http://www.cnn.com/2013/02/20/tech/web/hacked-apple-facebook-twitter/index.html.

[15] N. Perlroth, "Some Victims of Online Hacking Edge Into the Light," The New York Times, 20 February 2013. [Online]. Available: http://www.nytimes.com/2013/02/21/technology/hacking-victims-edge-into-light.html.

[16] S. Cowley, "FBI Director: Cybercrime will eclipse terrorism," CNNMoney, 2 March 2012. [Online]. Available: http://money.cnn.com/2012/03/02/technology/fbi_cybersecurity/index.htm.

[17] P. Hoonakker, N. Bornoe and P. Carayon, "Password Authentication from a Human Factors Perspective: Results of a Survey among End-Users," PROCEEDINGS of the HUMAN FACTORS and ERGONOMICS SOCIETY 53rd ANNUAL MEETING, 2009. [Online]. Available: http://www.hfes.org/web/Newsroom/HFES09-Hoonaker-CIS.pdf.

[18] M. Kotadia, "Microsoft security guru: Jot down your passwords," CNet, 23 May 2005. [Online]. Available: http://news.cnet.com/Microsoft-security-guru-Jot-down-your-passwords/2100-7355_3-5716590.html.

[19] R. Cheng and D. McCullagh, "Yahoo breach: Swiped passwords by the

numbers," CNet, 12 July 2012. [Online]. Available: http://news.cnet.com/8301-1009_3-57470878-83/yahoo-breach-swiped-passwords-by-the-numbers/.

[20] J. Timmer, "30 years of failure: the username/password combination," Ars Technica, 31 October 2009. [Online]. Available: http://arstechnica.com/business/2009/10/30-years-of-failure-the-user-namepassword-combination/.

[21] N. Anderson, "How I became a password cracker: Cracking passwords is officially a "script kiddie" activity now," Ars Technica, 24 March 2013. [Online]. Available: http://arstechnica.com/security/2013/03/how-i-became-a-password-cracker/.

[22] The LastPass Team, "LastPass Security Notification," LastPass, 4 May 2011. [Online]. Available: http://blog.lastpass.com/2011/05/lastpass-security-notification.html.

[23] D. Goodin, "Hack of cloud-based LastPass exposes hashed master passwords," Ars Technica, 15 June 2015. [Online]. Available: http://arstechnica.com/security/2015/06/hack-of-cloud-based-lastpass-exposes-encrypted-master-passwords/.

[24] D. Danchev, "Attacker: Hacking Sarah Palin's email was easy," ZDNet, 18 September 2008. [Online]. Available: http://www.zdnet.com/blog/security/attacker-hacking-sarah-palins-email-was-easy/1939.

[25] The Mad Dog, "tinkerbell hack," Urban Dictionary, 15 March 2010. [Online]. Available: http://www.urbandictionary.com/define.php?term=tinkerbell%20hack.

[26] A. Wawro, "How to set up two-factor authentication for Facebook, Google, Microsoft, and more," PCWorld, 25 April 2013. [Online]. Available: http://www.pcworld.com/article/2036252/how-to-set-up-two-factor-authentication-for-facebook-google-microsoft-and-more.html.

[27] Google, "About 2-step verification," Google, [Online]. Available: http://support.google.com/accounts/bin/answer.py?hl=en&answer=180744. [Accessed 10 May 2013].

[28] D. Merica, "Five things you need to know about U.S. national security," CNN, 29 July 2012. [Online]. Available: http://security.blogs.cnn.com/2012/07/29/five-things-you-need-to-know-about-u-s-national-security/.

[29] D. Goldman, "Watching porn is bad for your smartphone," CNNMoney, 11

February 2013. [Online]. Available: http://money.cnn.com/2013/02/11/technology/security/smartphone-porn/index.html.

[30] B. X. Chen, "Get Ready for 1 Billion Smartphones by 2016, Forrester Says," The New York Times, 13 February 2012. [Online]. Available: http://bits.blogs.nytimes.com/2012/02/13/get-ready-for-1-billion-smartphones-by-2016-forrester-says/.

[31] D. Goldman, "Your smartphone will (eventually) be hacked," CNNMoney, 12 September 2012. [Online]. Available: http://money.cnn.com/2012/09/17/technology/smartphone-cyberattack/index.html.

[32] "FCC Smartphone Security Checker," FCC, [Online]. Available: http://www.fcc.gov/smartphone-security. [Accessed 25 January 2013].

[33] A. Souppourison, "iPhone lockscreen can be bypassed with new iOS 6.1 trick," The Verge, 14 February 2013. [Online]. Available: http://www.theverge.com/2013/2/14/3987830/ios-6-1-security-flaw-lets-anyone-make-calls-from-your-iphone.

[34] B. Stone, "Google Says It Inadvertently Collected Personal Data," The New York Times, 14 May 2010. [Online]. Available: http://bits.blogs.nytimes.com/2010/05/14/google-admits-to-snooping-on-personal-data/.

[35] M. Landis, "Google admits to accidentally collecting e-mails, URLs, passwords," CNN, 22 October 2010. [Online]. Available: http://articles.cnn.com/2010-10-22/tech/google.privacy.controls_1_wifi-data-alan-eustace-google-s-street-view?_s=PM:TECH.

[36] A. Eustace, "Creating stronger privacy controls inside Google," Google Public Policy Blog, 22 October 2010. [Online]. Available: http://googlepublicpolicy.blogspot.com/2010/10/creating-stronger-privacy-controls.html.

[37] M. Jewell, "TJX breach could top 94 million accounts," NBC News, 24 October 2007. [Online]. Available: http://www.msnbc.msn.com/id/21454847/ns/technology_and_science-security/t/tjx-breach-could-top-million-accounts/.

[38] B. Sullivan, "ID theft on the rise again: 12.6 million victims in 2012, study shows," NBC News, 20 February 2013. [Online]. Available: http://redtape.nbcnews.com/_news/2013/02/20/17022584-id-theft-on-the-rise-again-126-million-victims-in-2012-study-shows.

[39] J. Pagliery, "Hospital network hacked, 4.5 million records stolen," CNNMoney, 18 August 2014. [Online]. Available: http://money.cnn.com/2014/08/18/technology/security/hospital-chs-hack/index.html.

[40] Federal Trade Commission, "About Identity Theft," Federal Trade Commission, [Online]. Available: http://www.ftc.gov/bcp/edu/microsites/idtheft/consumers/about-identity-theft.html. [Accessed 14 May 2012].

[41] Federal Bureau of Investigation, "Malware Installed on Travelers' Laptops Through Software Updates on Hotel Internet Connections," Federal Bureau of Investigation, 8 May 2012. [Online]. Available: http://www.fbi.gov/scams-safety/e-scams.

[42] A. Tuerk, "Giving you more insight into your Google Account activity," Google Official Blog, 28 March 2012. [Online]. Available: http://googleblog.blogspot.com/2012/03/giving-you-more-insight-into-your.html.

[43] Google Alerts, "What are Google Alerts?," Google, 25 May 2012. [Online]. Available: https://support.google.com/alerts/bin/answer.py?hl=en&answer=175925.

[44] N. Lee, "Facebook Nation: Total Information Awareness (2nd Edition)," Springer Science+Business Media, 14 October 2014. [Online]. Available: http://www.amazon.com/exec/obidos/ASIN/1493917390/creativehollywoo/.

[45] M. Honan, "How Apple and Amazon Security Flaws Led to My Epic Hacking," Wired, 6 August 2012. [Online]. Available: http://www.wired.com/gadgetlab/2012/08/apple-amazon-mat-honan-hacking/all/.

[46] N. Lee, "Counterterrorism and Cybersecurity: Total Information Awareness," Springer, 8 April 2015. [Online]. Available: http://www.amazon.com/exec/obidos/ASIN/3319172433/creativehollywoo/.

# Index

## 1
1Password, 13

## 2
2-step verification, 18

## A
Advanced Encryption Standard, 24
AES. *See* Advanced Encryption Standard
AFP. *See* Australian Federal Police
Alexander, Keith, 20
Alperovitch, Dmitri, 7
Amazon Top 500 reviewer, 17
anti-virus software, 26
Apple, 6
Apple iCloud, 18, 29
AppleID, 29
ArcelorMittal, 6
Asia, 23
associative memory, 11
Australian Federal Police, 4

## B
Baker Hughes, 6
Betty Boop, 11
BG Group, 6
BP, 6

## C
Canada, 23
Central Security Service, 20
Chesapeake Energy, 6
Chrome, 13
cloud computing, 29
Coca-Cola, 6
coffee shops, 23
collision resistance, 5, 14
common passwords, 8
ConocoPhillips, 6
credit freeze, 27
credit history, 25
cryptography, 7
cybercriminals, 4
cybersecurity, 30

## D
department stores, 23
dictionary words, 9, 10, 19
Dropbox, 18
Dunst, Kirsten, 6
Dutch National High Tech Crime Unit, 4

## E
encryption, 17
Equifax, 27
Europe, 23
Eustace, Alan, 23
Evernote, 5
Experian, 27
Exxon Mobil, 6

## F
Facebook, 6, 18, 28
*Facebook Nation*, 28
FCC. *See* Federal Communications Commission
Federal Bureau of Investigation, 6, 26
Federal Communications Commission, 20
Firefox, 13
firewalls, 4
Florida, 24

fraud alert, 27
FTC. *See* Federal Trade Commission

## G

Gmail, 29
Google, 15, 18, 29
Google Account Activity, 27
Google Alerts, 27
Google Maps, 23
Google Street View, 23
Guardians of Peace, 6

## H

hackers, 4
hash function, 5, 14
Hilton, Paris, 15
Honan, Mat, 29, 30
hotels, 26
**http**, 17
**https**, 17
Hypertext Transfer Protocol Secure, 17

## I

iCloud, 6
identity theft, 4, 25
International Olympic Committee, 6
Internet Explorer, 13
iPad, 29
iPhone, 29
Irish Reporting and Information Security Service, 4
IRISS. *See* Irish Reporting and Information Security Service

## J

jailbreaking, 21
Johansson, Jesper, 8, 12

## K

KeePass, 13
Kernell, David, 15
keyloggers, 13
keysniffers, 13

## L

LastPass, 13
Lawrence, Jennifer, 6
LinkedIn, 5, 14, 28
long passwords, 15, 19

## M

MacBook, 29
Marshalls, 24
master password, 13
McAfee, 20
Mexico, 23
Miami, 24
Microsoft, 8, 12, 18
Mueller, Robert, 6

## N

National Security Agency, 14
network administrators, 9
NHTCU. *See* Dutch National High Tech Crime Unit

## P

Palin, Sarah, 15
paperless statements, 26
password changes, 11
password leaf, 11
password manager, 13
password protection, 4
password security questions, 4, 15
password stem, 10

Password-Based Key Derivation Function 2, 13
PBKDF2. *See* Password-Based Key Derivation Function 2
PCeU. *See* U.K. Police Central e-Crime Unit
PlentyofFish.com, 5

## R

remote bricking, 22
remote wipe, 21
restaurants, 26
RockYou, 5, 17
Royal Dutch Shell, 6
RSA SecurID, 10
Russian roulette, 20

## S

Safari, 13
Secure Hash Algorithm, 14
selfie, 6
SHA. *See* Secure Hash Algorithm
SHA-1, 5, 14
SHA-2, 14
SHA-256, 14
shorthand, 12
smartphone, 20
Social Security number, 26
Sony Pictures, 6
stem-leaf password system, 10
strong passwords, 4, 10, 17

## T

Temporal Key Integrity Protocol, 24
Thompson, Hugh, 20
Tinkerbell, 15
tinkerbell hack, 15
TJX, 24
TKIP. *See* Temporal Key Integrity Protocol

TransUnion, 27
Twitter, 5, 6, 18, 28, 29
two-factor authentication, 18

## U

U.K. Police Central e-Crime Unit, 4
U.S. Cyber Command, 20
U.S. Federal Trade Commission, 26
U.S. Secret Service, 4
United States, 23
Upton, Kate, 6
USSS. *See* U.S. Secret Service

## V

Verizon RISK Team, 4
virtual screen keyboard, 13

## W

weak passwords, 8, 9
WiFi, 23
Wi-Fi, 21
WiFi network router, 24
Wikipedia, 15
Winning, Ethan A., 17
Winstead, Mary Elizabeth, 6
Wireless Protected Access, 24
Wireless Protected Access 2, 24
WPA. *See* Wireless Protected Access
WPA Pre-Shared Key, 24
WPA2. *See* Wireless Protected Access 2
WPA2 Pre-Shared Key, 24
WPA2-PSK. *See* WPA2 Pre-Shared Key
WPA-PSK. *See* WPA Pre-Shared Key

## Y

Yahoo! Voices, 5

# About the Author

**Newton Lee** graduated Summa Cum Laude from Virginia Tech with a B.S. and M.S. degree in Computer Science, and he earned a perfect GPA from Vincennes University with an A.S. degree in Electrical Engineering and an honorary doctorate in Computer Science.

He is the coauthor of *Disney Stories: Getting to Digital;* author of the "Total Information Awareness" book series including *Facebook Nation* and *Counterterrorism and Cybersecurity*; and coauthor/editor of the "Digital Da Vinci" series including *Computers in Music* and *Computers in the Arts and Sciences.* He is the creator of the "Read Me First" book series.

www.ingramcontent.com/pod-product-compliance
Lightning Source LLC
Chambersburg PA
CBHW071552170526
45166CB00004B/1640